ASBC HANDBOOK SERIES
Practical Guides for Beer Quality

FRESHNESS

Charles W. Bamforth
University of California, Davis

AMERICAN SOCIETY OF
Brewing Chemists

Front cover: Photo courtesy Valdas/Shutterstock.com.

Reference in this publication to a trademark, proprietary product, or company name is intended for explicit description only and does not imply approval or recommendation to the exclusion of others that may be suitable.

Library of Congress Control Number: 2016959796
International Standard Book Numbers:
Print: 978-1-881696-27-8
Mobi eBook: 978-1-881696-28-5

© 2017 by the American Society of Brewing Chemists

All rights reserved.
No portion of this book may be reproduced in any form, including photocopy, microfilm, information storage and retrieval system, computer database, or software, or by any means, including electronic or mechanical, without written permission from the publisher.

Printed in the United States of America on acid-free paper

American Society of Brewing Chemists
3340 Pilot Knob Road
St. Paul, Minnesota 55121, U.S.A.

For Liam Donald Bamforth

This Book and This Series

This is the third volume in a six-part series addressing quality issues of beer. There are, of course, a number of books and numerous articles that address such matters. This particular series might be viewed as a set of user manuals, much like the handbook that accompanies your car.

In each book I seek to address individual quality issues from a standpoint of

- the basic underpinning science (without getting too complex and grinding the grist too fine),
- the practicalities of the issue pertaining to brewing and its associated activities,
- quality assurance and quality control parameters, and
- a troubleshooting guide (or key control point summary).

Acknowledgment

I am very grateful to Emily Kultgen for her excellent artwork.

Contents

1. The Challenge of Flavor Instability 1
2. Flavor Changes That Can Occur in Beer 7
3. The Underpinning Science of Flavor Change 13
4. Evaluating Flavor Change: By Taste and Smell 25
5. Analytical Approaches to the Study of Flavor Instability................. 31
6. The Key Disagreement: How Important Is Upstream Oxidation?..... 39
7. Strategies for Minimizing Flavor Change.... 43
8. Light Instability: Skunking 51

Further Reading 55

Index.. 59

The Challenge of Flavor Instability

Chapter 1

They were auspicious days: a time when the British government was prepared to provide financial support for the brewing industry. I found myself in the corridors of power in the Ministry of Agriculture, Fisheries, and Food and in the office of a pin-striped career civil servant who might easily have stepped off the set of *Yes, Minister*.

"So what is the problem?" he sniffed.

"Well, it's all about the staling of beer," I replied.

"Tell me about it."

"The flavor of beer changes with time. Some of the good flavors are lost. Meanwhile some undesirable ones, like tomcat pee and cardboard, develop."

"I see," he sneered. "Tell me, do you put a 'best-before date' on the beer?"

I replied in the affirmative.

"It's usually 9 months," I volunteered.

"My word, quite a long time. Why set it at that?"

"Well, the brewer is pretty confident that in that time frame, it's not going to go cloudy or throw sediment. Customers hate seeing that. They think it means that something is growing in the beer, but that rarely happens these days."

Chapter 1

The Challenge of Flavor Instability

"I understand," he retorted. "But the beer can be on the shelf for several months and it's 'stale,' I guess you would call it. But people still buy it?"

I nodded.

"Then what is the problem?"

A lengthy pause followed as he peered intently at me and I, wide eyed, searched my innermost resources for a worthy riposte.

I'm not sure I had one—though it didn't matter, as the man had clearly decided he would sanction the funding no matter how seemingly weak my argument. It was only later when I was in a conversation with Tony Whitear, then the Research Director of Whitbread and the most genial of men, that he provided the obvious answer: because a customer should expect two samples of the same brand of beer bought close to one another, both in location and time, to taste the same. Imagine consuming a couple of bottles of the same brand side by side that taste differently. The customer would be confounded (assuming he or she noticed).

Strangely, it would seem, some people don't buy into this argument when it comes to beer. People who would be pretty irritated if they bought a couple of cans of minestrone soup and found that one of them contained no vegetables claim to be unfazed by the freshness of beer. I don't believe it—though the situation is certainly baffling at times, as I will now relate.

Consider a trial we did in 2001. One of my M.S. students, the affable Bill Stephenson, took bottles of a famous North American lager beer and placed them in the oven at 30°C (86°F) for a month, such that they were nicely cooked. Having cooled them back down, he took them and an unaged batch of the same beer into Sacramento, California (U.S.A.), and presented them to people. These people claimed to be beer drinkers, though they were not trained as such. Bill poured beers in pairs and distinguished them by placing the glasses on different beer mats. When he took a fresh sample of the beer (let's call it Beer B) and put it on a mat boasting the brand logo and compared it with a stale Beer B (also placed on a mat with the logo) and then asked people for their preferences, there was a 50:50 split. Half the tasters seemed to prefer the fresh B, and the other half the stale B. When Bill repeated this but put the beers on plain mats with no logos, he got exactly the same result. However, when he took the fresh Beer B and put it into both glasses—one on a branded mat, one a plain mat—there was a 2:1

Chapter 1

The Challenge of Flavor Instability

preference for the beer on the branded mat. With the stale B in both glasses, folks voted 2:1 for the one on the plain mat.

The head technical honcho of the company whose beer we used asked me, "Charlie, why did you do that?" and of course, my answer was "Freedom of academic curiosity." But the conclusion is clear: People are heavily swayed by branding, irrespective of freshness. They do notice cleanness of flavor, and if not persuaded by branding, they seem to prefer the less-stale product.

Another study, this one conducted by my colleague Jean-Xavier Guinard, further illustrates the issue. He presented people with imported and U.S. beers and found that they voted 2:1 for the imports—the perception being that beers shipped from time-honored brewing nations such as Belgium, Britain, and Germany are more authentic and somehow superior. Expert tasters identified the numerous aged flaws in these imports, but clearly, the tasters were not swayed by such defects (if faults they be—isn't the customer always right?). When Guinard had the beers tasted in a hidden, nonbranded format, there was no such preference.

We saw in the first book of this series, *Foam,* that people drink with their eyes and are heavily influenced by the foam. It seems that even before they pour the beer into a glass (assuming that they do this, the civilized thing), they have made big decisions simply on the basis of branding and provenance (Fig. 1-1). Dare I even suggest that similar conclusions are drawn by drinkers when presented with a beer brewed by a smaller brewing company as opposed to a very large one?

Despite these findings on imported beer, there remains an undercurrent of confusion in the mind of the customer. I have lost track of the number of times that people have said to me, "What is this beer (let's call it Beer H) supposed to taste like? I have just come back from Europe, and I had it on tap over there. It tastes nothing like it does in California." The answer, of course, is that the beer's flavor is intimately linked to how much oxidation has taken place in it and how much light it has seen.

When Bill Stephenson put this particular imported beer (Beer H) into his trial (the one with Beer B) and compared beer that had been exposed to bright sunlight with beer that had been kept in the dark, tasters seemed to have much less doubt. In every way that we made the comparison, tasters had a 2:1 preference for the nonskunked version. (This result also says, obviously, that one-third of the tasters liked skunky flavor.)

Chapter 1

The Challenge of Flavor Instability

Fig. 1-1. Qualities such as foam, branding, and national origin influence customers before they have even tasted a beer. (Courtesy EcoPim Studio/Shutterstock.com)

Here is another tale: At the time that I was Quality Assurance Manager for the Preston Brook Brewery of Bass (England), we were one of several plants that brewed Carling Black Label—the biggest brand in the U.K. and a beer for whom the "mother ship" was Burton. (Everyone's Carling had to match that from Burton.) Each month, we were required to send a batch of our beer to HQ for comparison with samples from other locations. And every time, we were criticized for a distinct grainy character displayed by our version. "Clean it up" came the call to me and the Head Brewer, Neil Talbot. We did: I believe we changed the wet-milling regime, tinkered with the extent to which we

Chapter 1
The Challenge of Flavor Instability

collected last runnings, and improved the vigor of the boil. Now, we had a great match with the rest of the group—and now, our beer started to be complained about in the marketplace. The customers liked what we **had** been serving them!

This was an issue with the fresh beer, but the same argument surely applies when it comes to changes introduced by aging. Notwithstanding our earlier finding with Beer B, you will find that if a beer is perceived by the drinker as being different from the one they expect, then they will complain. And so if they are used to an aged beer—say, perhaps because it has traversed the oceans—then that is a note that they expect to see. I recall one prominent scientist from South Africa suggesting that perhaps the best thing to do would be to cook the beer in the brewery on the basis that it will never get worse and its flavor will be sealed, as it were.

One thing is for sure: The problem of flavor change can be much more of an issue with the gentler-nuanced beers. They will reveal the appearance of an off flavor more obviously and probably sooner than a beer of intense character. However, equally, perhaps the loss of a character is more obvious in a more fully flavored beer. For example, if a beer is noted for its hop aroma, the diminution of that character may be very transparent. Some very intensely flavored beers (for example, West Coast IPAs) can change flavor relatively rapidly.

A further complication is this: Flavor change might actually benefit some beers, much as winemakers speak of "laying down wines" for them to mature. It should come as no surprise that the beers most likely to benefit from some aging are those of higher alcohol content (such as barley wines) and those with the highest tannin content. The alcohol molecules likely react with other components of the beer to produce interesting aroma notes. Meanwhile, oxidative reactions will lead to polymerization of the polyphenols and an attendant decrease in astringency.

Unlike other aspects of beer quality (as discussed in the other volumes in this series), for flavor stability, the situation is not clear-cut. It is generally the case that customers will be unequivocal about whether beer should have a head on it, whether it should be bright or turbid, and what color it should be. But when it comes to whether fresh beer or stale beer is the more desirable, there is confusion, simply because clearly there are those folks who actually like the very characteristics that most brewers deplore (such as cardboard, tomcat pee, and so on).

Chapter 1

The Challenge of Flavor Instability

Yet I maintain my own conviction that what we should aspire to is **consistency:** If a beer displays stale character and that is the note the customer has become used to sensing in his or her beer, then for goodness sake, render it always thus (although I personally believe that stale beer is less drinkable)! To take an extreme example, a devotee of spontaneously fermented beers, with their profound funky character, would be appalled to find his or her favorite brew devoid of sublime sourness and bountiful barnyard.

In volume 2 of this series, *Flavor*, we focused on achieving consistency in newly packaged beers. In this volume, we will focus on the stability of that flavor.

Flavor Changes That Can Occur in Beer

Chapter 2

If you were simply to believe the burgeoning literature on flavor instability in beer, you might almost believe that the only significant change that takes place as beer ages is the development of a **cardboard** (wet paper) note. So, much of the focus over the years has been on ascertaining what causes this character, how it develops, and how to delay it from happening. The consensus has emerged that it's due to a molecule called *E-2-nonenal* (which used to be called *trans-2-nonenal*), that it develops as a result of the oxidation of unsaturated fatty acids through the agency of an enzyme called *lipoxygenase,* and that if you kill off that enzyme, you will buy shelf life. The reality is that nonenal is but one of the sources of the cardboard character, that lipoxygenase represents just one route by which it can be made, and most importantly of all, that cardboard is but one of the myriad of flavor changes that characterize beer aging. You will not sort out flavor change by focusing on the nonenal story alone.

One of the first efforts to put words to the changes that take place when beer ages can be ascribed to Charles Dalgliesh in 1977, erstwhile Director of the then Brewing Research Foundation. He described a decrease in bitterness and a concomitant increase in sweetness, although it is not clear whether these are independent phenomena as perceived by expert tasters or a decrease in **perceived** apparent bitterness because the increase in sweetness confuses tasters. Alternatively, it might be

Chapter 2
Flavor Changes That Can Occur in Beer

the converse, with a reduced bitterness manifesting itself as increased sweetness. As we will see, there is no disputing that the level of bitter acids in beer does indeed decrease during beer storage. Furthermore, the perception of sweetness may manifest itself in descriptors such as *caramel, burnt sugar,* and *toffee-like* and may indeed represent genuine development of these notes. Dalgliesh also described the development and subsequent subsiding of a ribes character—which is politely described as *black currant buds/leaves* and less pleasantly, perhaps, as *tomcat urine*—and the development of the cardboard or wet paper aroma that so captivates most researchers.

It is salutary, however, to appreciate that this description is nothing more than an approximate summation of the overall changes that occurred in the ale that were featured in that particular study. And so, for example, legendary sensory scientist Morten Meilgaard declared that the development of a cardboard aroma as beer ages is followed by a **decrease** in that character.

Plenty of other notes have been described in aged beer. (For example, take a look at the paper I wrote with Sarah Bushnell and Jean-Xavier Guinard; see "Further Reading" at the end of the book and also Sidebar 2-1 in this chapter.) Different scientists have variously reported harsh after-bitter and astringent tastes, wine- and whiskey-like aromas, and bready, toffee-like, honey, earthy, woody, hay or straw-like, and burnt or licorice tastes. Characters that are well known as being important for the flavor of fresh beers, such as fruity/estery and floral, may decrease in intensity—a phenomenon that is no less flavor instability than is the development of "new" notes.

Other examples might include the development of a diacetyl character in beer, wherein the acetolactate precursor was not properly eliminated during fermentation (see volume 2) and the scalping of hop oils on crown cork liners as bottled beer is stored. The list is seemingly endless. **Any change that can be perceived by nose or taste that shifts a beer away from its avowed flavor profile represents flavor instability.** Considering that there are literally hundreds and hundreds of flavor-active substances in beer and that they can be perceived at extremely low levels in many instances, then the problem of flavor instability is manifestly challenging. Let me say again: Focusing on just one thing, such as lipoxygenase, is not of itself going to solve the staling conundrum.

Sidebar 2-1. Training a Panel to Assess the Staling of Beer[1]

The development of a properly trained panel is not a trivial task. A study by Bushnell et al. (2003) involved looking at the relative importance of sulfur dioxide (SO_2) and polyphenols to staling. However, the aim here is to illustrate how a study should be performed and reported, not the precise outcome of this particular investigation.

Preliminary Tasting

A preliminary tasting was held to profile the samples that the panel would evaluate. This tasting allowed for standards to be presented in the first panel session and provided some direction to the panel. The samples employed in the tasting were representative of those the panel used for term generation and training. Prepared in the American ale and lager were a fresh sample aged at 60°C (86°F) for 24 hr, a sample aged at 40°C (104°F) for 24 hr, and a sample in which 20 ppm of SO_2 was added 24 hr prior to tasting. The American ale and lager were packaged in brown glass. The ale was approximately 2 months old at evaluation, and the lager was 3 weeks old. A principal component analysis (PCA) was not done on the combined SO_2 and polyvinyl polypyrrolidone (PVPP) data set.

Panel

A panel of 11 judges—eight men and three women between the ages of 22 and 27 and all with brewing or sensory experience—was assembled. Judges were compensated for their participation. During term generation and training, panelists attended two 1-hr sessions per week. During data collection, panelists attended three 15- to 30-min sessions per week.

Term Generation and Scorecard Development

Seven term-generation sessions were held. Beers selected for term generation were similar to those that would be evaluated in the experiment. References for the sensory attributes were developed and presented to the panel, beginning with the first session. The references presented in the first term-generation session were based on the outcome of the preliminary tasting. Lager and ale sessions were held during alternate weeks. The preliminary list of terms, encompassing both beer types, covered aroma and taste characteristics of the beers.

Training

Six training sessions were held initially. During training, group rankings were used in which the panel decided as a group which samples were highest and lowest in each attribute. Group consensus ratings were also used, in which the panel decided as a group on a score for each attribute. Individual ratings were performed to monitor individual progress. Retraining sessions were held as necessary after breaks from data collection. In the retraining sessions, panelists were given high and low reference samples.

The panelists narrowed down and combined terms from the term-generation phase to yield a scorecard with 11 attributes (Table 2-1). This scorecard was created to evaluate the lager and ale samples. The scorecard used a scale of 0 to 10. The values were not anchored.

References were made for all 11 attributes (Table 2-2). The aroma standards were made 2 hr before evaluation and were presented at room temperature. The taste standards were made 1 hr before evaluation and were served cold in 60-mL (2-ounce) translucent plastic cups. Aroma standards were presented throughout term generation, training, retraining, and data collection. Taste standards were presented only during term generation, training, and retraining.

Assessment of Judge Performance Upon Training

To determine the panel's readiness for descriptive data collection, a set of samples was evaluated in duplicate over two sessions. Analysis of variance (ANOVA)

---
[1] Adapted, by permission, from Bushnell et al. (2003).

Sidebar 2-1. continued

TABLE 2-1. Aroma and flavor attributes selected for descriptive analysis and corresponding descriptors[a]

Attribute	Descriptors
Hops aroma	Earthy, floral, green, herbal
Canned-corn aroma	Buttery, vegetal, sulfurous
Cardboard aroma	Musty, dusty, stale, papery, flat
Malt/Molasses/Roasted/Toasted aroma	Sweet, grainy, nutty, burnt
Hay/Straw aroma	Barnyard, dry field
Apple/Wine aroma	Sweet, alcoholic, esters, white wine (Riesling)
Bitter flavor	Back of the throat, aftertaste, lingering
Canned-corn flavor	Butter, cooked veggie, aftertaste
Cardboard flavor	Dull, stale, bland, flat
Malt/Molasses/Roasted/Toasted flavor	Dry sweetness, grainy, nutty, burnt
Apple/Wine flavor	Sweet, sour, alcohol, Riesling

[a] Adapted, by permission, from Bushnell et al. (2003).

was applied to the ratings, and the criteria of judge performance were monitored as follows:
- Significant F-ratios for the samples were taken as indicators of the panel's ability to discriminate among the samples.
- F-ratios for the replications and the judge by replication interaction were examined for panel reproducibility.
- Concept alignment was assessed with the F-ratios for the judge by sample interaction.

These criteria of judge performance were met to the experimenters' satisfaction, and the panel was deemed ready for the actual descriptive analysis.

Experimental Design and Procedure

All samples were evaluated in triplicate by the panel. Each sample was labeled with a random three-digit code generated from a Latin square presentation design. The products to be evaluated were split into blocks for evaluation based on beer type (lager or ale) and treatment (SO_2 or PVPP, with controls in each case). Samples were held in a cooler at 0°C (32°F) until the day before evaluation, when they were transferred to a refrigerator at 4°C (39°F). Samples were poured just before evaluation and presented monadically. Each bottle was held on ice and used for 30 min or less before a new bottle was opened. The samples were served in dark-blue glasses to mask potential visual differences.

The descriptive analysis was conducted in individual booths illuminated with incandescent lighting using the FIZZ Network Acquisition software (produced by Biosystemes) for data collection. Judges rinsed with drinking water between samples and were given the option to expectorate.

Aging Regimens

An aging regimen of 60°C (140°F) for 24 hr was used during term generation and training. Aging for the SO_2 and PVPP trials was at 30°C (86°F) for 30 days.

By using difference testing, it was determined that the panel could differentiate the two aging regimens in the ale but not in the lager. However, in the descriptive

Sidebar 2-1. continued

TABLE 2-2. Aroma and flavor terms selected for descriptive analysis and composition of corresponding reference standards[a]

Term	Composition of Reference Standard[b]
Hops aroma	5 cones of Saaz hops
Canned-corn aroma	1.5 mL (0.05 ounce) of S&W whole-kernel-corn brine
Cardboard aroma	30 mL (1 ounce) of the lager beer used in data collection aged at 60°C (140°F) for 24 hr
Malt/Molasses/Roasted/Toasted aroma	5 kernels of crystal malt, 1 drop of Brer Rabbit full-flavor molasses, a pinch of toasted bread crumbs
Hay/Straw aroma	5 pieces of straw
Apple/Wine aroma	1 g (0.04 ounce) of Red Delicious apple, 1 g of Granny Smith apple, 4 mL (0.14 ounce) of Carlos Rossi Chablis white table wine
Bitter flavor	2 drops of isomerized hop extract
Canned-corn flavor	15 mL (0.5 ounce) of S&W whole-kernel-corn brine
Cardboard flavor	Lager beer used in data collection aged at 60°C (140°F) for 24 hr
Malt/Molasses/Roasted/Toasted flavor	3 g (0.11 ounce) of crystal malt, 2.5 mL (0.8 ounce) of Brer Rabbit full-flavor molasses, 10 g (0.4 ounce) of roasted corn, 2 g (0.07 ounce) of toasted bread crumbs
Apple/Wine flavor	10 g (0.4 ounce) of Red Delicious apple, 10 g of Granny Smith apple, 45 mL (1.5 ounces) of Carlos Rossi Chablis white table wine

[a] Adapted, by permission, from Bushnell et al. (2003).
[b] Aroma and flavor standards are made in 30 and 355 mL (1 and 12 ounces), respectively, of an American lager beer. Exceptions are noted.

analysis, the panelists used the same terms to describe aged beer characteristics irrespective of the temperature regimen employed. We agree with others that while accelerated aging is imperfect, it is sufficiently reliable and realistic for investigations of the current type, particularly at the lower of the two temperatures.

Statistical Analysis

An individual ANOVA was run on each attribute rated by the judges using the Statistical Analysis System (SAS) software (produced by SAS Institute). The products were split into four blocks by beer type (lager or ale) and treatment (SO_2 or PVPP). Fisher's least significant difference (LSD) test was used to examine differences among means.

Chapter 2

Flavor Changes That Can Occur in Beer

To add to the complexity, the precise flavor notes observed also seem to depend on the aging conditions (Fig. 2-1). Ribes is strongly correlated with the amount of oxygen in a package, while higher storage temperatures (for example, of the type used in accelerated aging experiments; see Chapter 4) tend to exaggerate the cardboard character, which is perhaps one of the reasons why that particular aroma note is focused on so heavily in research that typically force-ages beer prior to tasting. In beer held at the temperature at which most beer is normally stored, there is a rather limited increase in the E-2-nonenal level, and some folks have even reported that the level can decrease.

By now, the reader will have surmised that we are dealing with an extremely complicated problem. For as many flavor substances as are present in beer or that can develop in beer over time, there is an added level of complexity.

In the next chapter, we will search for some clues as to the nature of these flavor changes and the factors that may be relevant in their development.

Fig. 2-1. Storage temperature is one of the key conditions that affects how beer ages. (Courtesy Cheryl Casey/Shutterstock.com)

The Underpinning Science of Flavor Change

Chapter 3

As we ascertained in Chapter 2, a change in the perceptible level of any of the hundreds of substances that can contribute to the flavor of beer represents flavor instability. Furthermore, some of these substances can be detected at extremely low levels—that is, they have very low *flavor thresholds.* (See volume 2 for an explanation of what this term means.) Therefore, the likelihood of perceiving a change in aroma and/or taste is extremely high.

Remember that this may be due to a decrease in flavor—for instance, bitterness, esteriness, or hoppiness. Or it may be due to the appearance of a note—such as woody, straw, or cardboard.

The challenge to the brewer, then, is unmistakable. He or she cannot hope to pick off the substances one by one. Rather, the brewer must look for general approaches that are likely to, at a sweep, minimize the extent to which all the changes happen. In short, we need to look for generalities: whatever we can discover that is common among as many of these substances as possible. And one such commonality is the presence of carbonyl groups. (It is not the intention of this series of books to dwell too heavily on chemistry, but sometimes, bits and pieces are unavoidable!)

The carbonyl group comprises a carbon atom linked to an oxygen atom through two attachments (bonds). Hence, it is a so-called double bond, and chemically, we represent carbonyl as follows:

$C=O$

Chapter 3

The Underpinning Science of Flavor Change

This group is present in a great many of the substances that impact beer flavor. To take just a few, they include diacetyl (*butterscotch, popcorn*), acetaldehyde (*green apple*), and E-2-nonenal (*cardboard*). We discussed the first two of these at length in volume 2 of this series. Here, let us consider nonenal and other carbonyl-containing products.

A range of wort and beer components can degrade to produce carbonyl-containing entities. If you peruse the scientific literature, you will find folks who champion certain routes toward staling and cast doubt on the significance of others. It all adds to the complexity!

Oxidation of Unsaturated Fatty Acids

Let's start with the one that everyone seems to focus on: namely, the oxidation of the so-called unsaturated fatty acids. These acids originate in barley, and the most important one is linoleic acid. Linoleic acid molecules react with oxygen to produce oxidized fatty acids. We have encountered these before, in volume 1, for they are foam negative. However, they are also susceptible to being broken down to produce E-2-nonenal, which as we have seen, does indeed have a cardboard character.

Unsaturated fatty acids can be oxidized two ways. The first involves an enzyme called *lipoxygenase,* which we will abbreviate as LOX. This enzyme is not found in raw barley, but it does develop in the embryo of barley as germination proceeds. Because it is the embryo in which the bulk of the lipid is located, LOX can exert its impact during the sprouting process, resulting in the production of oxidized fatty acids (and this is enough to convince some brewers that the blame for a lack of freshness in their beer should be laid at the door of the maltster—but things are not so simple, as we will see). The more extensive the modification, the more LOX will develop.

LOX is an enzyme that does not care for heat, and it is extensively degraded during the kilning of malt. The more severely malt is dried, the more substantial the loss of LOX. So, a lightly dried pilsner malt will retain rather more LOX than a pale ale malt.

This heat susceptibility of LOX means that it will be destroyed much more rapidly in an infusion mash at, say, 65°C (149°F) than in a temperature-ramped mash, where it can work for longer at a low temperature start (say, 45°C [113°F]). Therefore, there are those that argue that the best scenario involves the highest practical mashing-in temperature for a malt that is kilned to the highest possible temperature commensurate with all other requirements (for example, color). In a nutshell, single-temperature infusion mashes are preferable to decoction mashes in this context, especially as the latter increase the risk of picking up oxygen with all that schlepping around.

It has been argued that not only polyphenols but also Maillard reaction products (the molecules produced by reacting sugars and amino acids together in kilning, leading to color formation) can inhibit LOX.

Even if no LOX survives, however, unsaturated fatty acids can still be oxidized. Such oxidation depends on the production of very active forms of oxygen called *reactive oxygen species* (ROS) (Fig. 3-1). ROS are generated from oxygen in various ways but most notably through interaction with iron, copper, and manganese. (They can also be produced through the agency of light, but then the more significant flavor impact is going to be skunkiness; see Chapter 8.) What happens is that these

Chapter 3

The Underpinning Science of Flavor Change

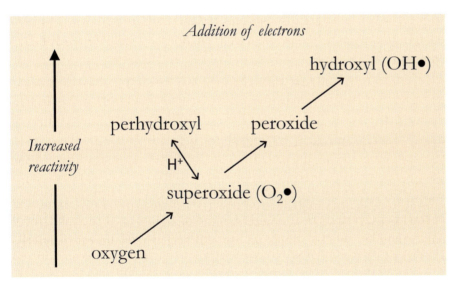

Fig. 3-1. Reactive oxygen species. Oxygen (O_2) is converted into progressively more damaging forms by picking up electrons from metal ions, such as iron, copper, and manganese. Superoxide can exist in two forms, depending on the pH. At pHs above 4.8, it is mostly as superoxide. At pHs below 4.8, it is mostly as the more damaging perhydroxyl. This is likely the reason that the lower the pH of the beer, the more rapidly it stales. (Each black dot indicates the presence of a spare electron. If you are a nonchemist, don't worry about it!) (Drawing by Emily Kultgen; Adapted from Bamforth [2006], Fig. 102)

Chapter 3

The Underpinning Science of Flavor Change

ROS react with the linoleic acid and convert it into a form that will react with oxygen to produce another reactive species (Fig. 3-2). This one reacts with another linoleic acid to form an oxidized fatty acid, at the same time making another reactive linoleic acid derivative—and so the cycle continues such that eventually, more and more of the linoleic acid is converted into the oxidized form that breaks down to produce nonenal.

The reader will have surmised that elimination of oxygen will prevent either route (enzymic or nonenzymic). It is not realistic to think of grain that does not contain lipid, but who needs oxygen in a mash? We will revisit this in Chapter 6.

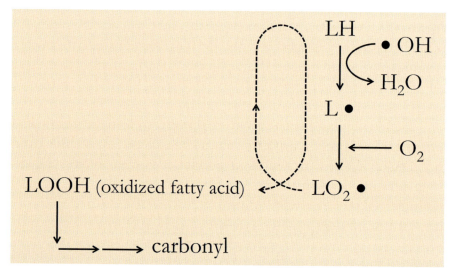

Fig. 3-2. Nonenzymic oxidation of unsaturated fatty acids. A very reactive species, such as hydroxyl (–OH•; see Fig. 3-1), can pull a hydrogen atom away from an unsaturated fatty acid (LH). This means that LH now has a free electron (hence, L•). It combines with another molecule of oxygen to form another reactive species (LO$_2$•), which is powerful enough to pull another H• from another unsaturated fatty acid, thereby making an oxidized fatty acid that can break down to a staling carbonyl. But note that by LO$_2$• grabbing a hydrogen, it has made another L•, which can go through the cycle again. In other words, as long as the cascade has been started by a low level of an activated species, such as hydroxyl (or perhydroxyl; see Fig. 3-1), then the unsaturated fatty acid will be manifestly oxidized by oxygen. Not an enzyme in sight! (Drawing by Emily Kultgen; Courtesy C. W. Bamforth)

Oxidation of Bitter Acids

As we saw in Chapter 2, the bitterness of beer decreases with time. This is a direct result of the instability of the iso-α-acids derived from hops. It might be supposed that this would be more evident to the taster in a more heavily bittered beer. The degradation of the bitter acids is not only an issue of losing bitterness; it also results in the formation of carbonyl staling substances.

The bitter acids, of course, occur in two forms: the so-called *cis* and *trans* forms (again, see volume 2 of this series), and their levels depend on how the iso-α-acids are produced—for example, whether by traditional boiling or by the isomerization processes employed in the manufacture of extracts. The *trans* isomers are much more prone to breakdown than the *cis* isomers, and their stability is least at lower pHs.

Oxidation of Alcohols

Higher alcohols (such as 2-methylpropanol, 2-methylbutanol, 3-methylbutanol, and 2-phenylethanol) can be oxidized to aldehydes (carbonyl compounds). This process is promoted by melanoidins: the colored substances produced during malt kilning. Again, this is more prevalent at lower pHs. Some brewing scientists claim that polyphenols inhibit this reaction.

Maillard Reaction Products

The melanoidins are, of course, produced in the Maillard reaction, as stated earlier. A vast array of substances are produced in this reaction, not only the colored materials. Among them are furfural and 5-hydroxymethylfurfural, which are associated with aged character, and their levels seem to be in proportion to the extent of heating that occurs, including in wort boiling. However, some brewing scientists claim that these sorts of reactions can occur in beer—especially beer stored at insufficiently low temperatures.

Melanoidins have variously been claimed to promote staling (see the earlier discussion of higher alcohol oxidation) and to inhibit staling

Chapter 3

The Underpinning Science of Flavor Change

(by scavenging reactive oxygen species)! Are you starting to get the feeling that avoiding flavor change is going to be a toughie?

Amino Acid Degradation

Amino acids can interact with some of the intermediates in browning reactions to produce carbonyl substances. In this instance, it is said that polyphenols can promote these reactions. Yes, that's right: Polyphenols can promote certain reactions that lead to flavor change, such as this one, but can inhibit others, such as higher alcohol oxidation. Another legendary brewing scientist, Joe Owades, showed that most of the oxygen absorbed in a beer is captured by polyphenols, identifying them as the number-one trap for this damaging commodity.

But That's Not All!

The previous discussion provides just a snapshot of some of the likely chemistry. Many other substances are known to change in level as beer ages, and nobody is entirely sure of the reactions that are involved.

To add to the complexity, the carbonyl products from these various reactions can interact to form different carbonyl-containing compounds. For instance, heptanal and acetaldehyde can interact to produce E-2-nonenal. This type of reaction is catalyzed by proline, which is the one protein degradation product (it is actually strictly an imino acid, rather than an amino acid) that is not utilized by yeast in brewery fermentations and that occurs in plentiful amounts in beer.

It is worth restating here that we should not worry only about carbonyl-containing substances when we consider flavor instability. To take just one example, consider the esters. Some of these increase in level during aging, whereas others decrease. Where does it all end?!

A Search for Common Denominators

As we have seen, scientists get very hung up about the relative significance of the previously described reactions to flavor instability.

Frankly, wherever the truth lies, it probably won't help in the quest to produce stable beer. For example, let's say that the higher alcohol breakdown route really is very important. What are you going to do about it? Eliminate higher alcohols? That would be tough to do, and it would be impossible if you factor in higher alcohols' direct influence on flavor and indirect impact as substrates in the production of esters. Eliminate the melanoidins? Come on, now!

And let's say that we did find a way to conquer this alcohol oxidation problem. We would have to do the same thing with, say, the bitterness breakdown problem. Then we would have to turn to the amino acid issues and so on. Are we going to successfully pick off these issues one at a time? I think not, because the chemistry of wort and beer is so very, very complex that we really can't hope to tackle it all from a flavor instability perspective.

As we will see in the next volume, which will delve into the clarity of beer, if we want to prevent beer from going cloudy, we can address all the components that cause the problem without any adverse effect on other aspects of beer quality. But we can't just exclude bitterness from the wort and beer—or higher alcohols or amino acids or other precursors. Furthermore, the haze-forming materials manifest their impact at relatively high concentrations. Staling, by contrast, is caused by materials that are detected at extremely low levels.

So, we must continue our search for common denominators: factors that are likely to impact the totality of flavor change that occurs.

Chapter 3

The Underpinning Science of Flavor Change

Oxygen

Nobody would argue the fact that the lower the oxygen content of a packaged beer, the more stable it will be. Oxidation reactions are very significant when it comes to flavor instability, as we have seen—either reactions directly involving oxygen (such as the oxidation of unsaturated fatty acids) or reactions in which relatively oxidizing conditions promote the reactions but the precise oxidizing agent is not oxygen directly. (Oxidation of higher alcohols is an example; see Sidebar 3-1.)

As we will see, a growing number of people believe that it is just as necessary to exclude oxygen upstream in the brewing process if freshness is to be maximized. We will explore this further in Chapter 6.

Sidebar 3-1. Oxidation and Reduction

The simplest way to consider oxidation is that it's what occurs when something reacts with a molecule of oxygen (O_2). However (and the nonchemists are just going to have to trust me on this), oxidation can also be thought of as the removal of hydrogen.

The opposite of oxidation is *reduction*. So this is either the removal of oxygen or the addition of hydrogen.

Figure 3-3 gives a simple illustration of this. As one molecule becomes oxidized, so something else becomes reduced.

If the nonchemists will accept another truth from me, then oxidation can also be considered to be a *loss* of electrons, whereas reduction is a *gain* of electrons. Figure 3-4 illustrates the concept of so-called redox chains.

So the argument goes that if oxygen has entered a system (say, wort), then it will have altered the so-called redox state (Fig. 3-5). It will have caused some molecules to have become oxidized. Even though there is no oxygen present, there are still materials that are capable of carrying out oxidation. This is what some scientists argue occurs in beer (and see Chapter 6 for a fuller description of this): that the ingress of oxygen into wort causes the oxidation of molecules that then carry the oxidative force downstream. One favored example is thiol-containing substances (Fig. 3-6).

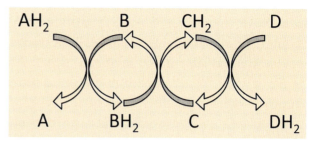

Fig. 3-4. A cascade of redox reactions. (Drawing by Emily Kultgen; Courtesy C. W. Bamforth)

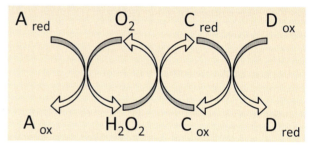

Fig. 3-5. How the oxidizing power of oxygen is transferred onward. (Drawing by Emily Kultgen; Courtesy C. W. Bamforth)

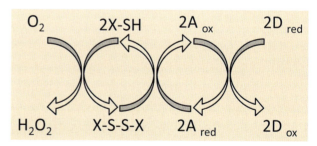

Fig. 3-6. Thiols (–SH) as carriers of oxidizing potential. (Drawing by Emily Kultgen; Courtesy C. W. Bamforth)

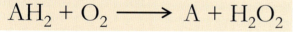

$$AH_2 + O_2 \longrightarrow A + H_2O_2$$

Fig. 3-3. A simple form of oxidation. Oxygen here is the oxidizing species, and AH_2 is the reducing species. In turn, the oxygen becomes reduced and the AH_2 becomes oxidized. (Drawing by Emily Kultgen; Courtesy C. W. Bamforth)

Metal Ions

We saw in the case of lipid oxidation that the most damaging species that kick off the breakdown process are reactive oxygen species (ROS). So, in addition to minimizing the amount of oxygen in beer, it is necessary to have as low levels of iron, copper, and manganese as possible.

Temperature

Swedish chemist Svante August Arrhenius (1859–1927) was 30 years old when he came up with the equation that relates the rate of a chemical reaction to temperature (Fig. 3-7). Simply put, for every 10°C in-

Fig. 3-7. Svante August Arrhenius. (Courtesy Zeitschrift für Physikalische Chemie, Band 69, von 1909)

Chapter 3

The Underpinning Science of Flavor Change

crease in temperature, a reaction will proceed two to three times more quickly. (The factor differs between reactions: Some will go at closer to double the speed but others at nearer three times the rate.) This equation applies just as much to the chemistry of beer aging as to anything else (see Table 3-1).

The "classic" room temperature is 20°C (68°F). There is a well-known brand of beer that proudly boasts a born-on date and advises that it's best drunk in less than 110 days from that date. This time frame was derived using Arrhenius's equation (assuming that the beer isn't going to be stored cold). But if beer is refrigerated, you can see immediately what a huge benefit this has for freshness. Equally, you can see the damage that can be caused by storing beer under warm conditions.

In research on beer aging, it is customary to speed up experiments by force-aging at increased temperature—and this is traditionally either 30°C (86°F) for 1 month or 60°C (140°F) for 1 day. You can see where these numbers come from.

As we have already said, the nature of flavor change differs depending on temperature, with cardboard character becoming prevalent at higher temperatures. Clearly, this occurs because of those different factors within the range of 2 to 3 times. Probably, the factor is 3 times for the production of nonenal but perhaps only 2 times for the production of, say, a wine-like character.

Table 3-1.

The impact of temperature on the staling of beer[a]

Temperature (°C)	Temperature (°F)	Days to Unacceptable Flavor
0	32	900
10	50	300
20	68	100
30	86	33
40	104	11
50	122	3–4
60	140	≈1

[a] I am assuming a factor of 3, as per Arrhenius: that is, reactions proceed three times faster for every 10°C increase in temperature and three times slower for every 10°C decrease in temperature.

Sulfites

If you take a stale beer and add enough sodium metabisulfite to it, then you can clean up the flavor. This speaks to the fact that sodium metabisulfite binds carbonyl substances to produce so-called adducts, which no longer display the aged character. This is a reversible reaction, so if the sulfite is removed, the carbonyl is released (Fig. 3-8).

David Ilett and Bill Simpson (1995) showed that this loss of sulfite occurs progressively in beer—especially if beer is stored warm! Even so, there is no question that metabisulfite can "buy" shelf life. The issue in the United States is that the label must declare "Contains sulfites" if there is more than 10 ppm of total sulfur dioxide in the beer.

$$\text{Carbonyl} + SO_2 \rightleftharpoons \text{Adduct}$$

Fig. 3-8. Adduct formation. (Drawing by Emily Kultgen; Courtesy C. W. Bamforth)

Chapter 3

The Underpinning Science of Flavor Change

Evaluating Flavor Change: By Taste and Smell

Chapter 4

Legendary brewing sensory scientist Morten Meilgaard wrote this in 2001 (Fig. 4-1):

Although the requirements for valid flavor assessment are well known, brewers fail to insist on their application. Of several hundred papers consulted, only two or three measure up.

In the lengthy critique he made of conclusions drawn on the basis of "dodgy" sensory work, he said, in the context of freshness:

Elaborate techniques to exclude oxygen during mashing, milling and lautering are harmless though hardly worth any extra cost.

More on this specific point in Chapter 6, but here we must linger a while on Meilgaard's main argument: that it is alarming indeed that so many "truths" seem to have become brewing "facts" that are founded on dubious sensory work. Perhaps nowhere is this more prevalent than in the study of flavor instability.

We talked at length about sensory techniques and conditions in volume 2 of this series (*Flavor*), and all of those considerations apply here. Rather than dwell on the minutiae of these matters again, let's focus on the generalities of applying the sensory tools to understanding flavor life.

Chapter 4

Evaluating Flavor Change: By Taste and Smell

Fig. 4-1. Morten Meilgaard (left) with Greg Casey, creator of the famous Fishbone diagrams (http://fishbones.asbcnet.org), in Toluca, Mexico in 1998. (Courtesy Greg Casey)

To start, let's consider how most people have approached investigations of flavor instability. They have a trial beer and a control beer. (A simple example is a trial beer containing an added antioxidant compared with a control without that antioxidant.) To accelerate the aging process, the beers are held at either 30°C (86°F) for 4 weeks or 60°C (140°F) for 1 day (see Chapter 3). Then the beer is tasted and scored for the intensity of its aged character. It might be assessed on a scale of 1 to 5, where 1 is "fresh" and 5 is "extremely stale." Table 4-1 gives a hypothetical example of how the data are often presented. The investigator would duly report that Antioxidant B is really exciting, and folks everywhere would start jumping up and down with exhilaration.

Table 4-1.

A typical manner by which people doing experiments on flavor stability report data

Treatment	Staleness Score
Control	4.1
Antioxidant A	3.9
Antioxidant B	2.7
Antioxidant C	3.3
Antioxidant D	4.3

Let's delve a bit deeper, though.

First, several questions must be asked: How many tasters were there, and how often did they taste the beers? What is the scatter on the data? Just how much overlap is there? What are the significant differences between the numbers, if any?

If those numbers are really for the control 4.1 ± 0.6 and Antioxidant B 2.7 ± 1.1, then things aren't quite so clear-cut, because in the extreme, we could have 3.5 for the control (as one of the extremes of the range for that value—i.e., 4.1 − 0.6) and 3.8 for Antioxidant B. And if the individual data are published from the various tasters and we find that the most gifted tasters are much more consistent than the others and score the control as 3.8 ± 0.2 and the Antioxidant B beer as 3.5 ± 0.2, then we can hardly say there is any difference.

Second, how often was the experiment done? How consistent are the observations across multiple trials with suitable controls? I believe that all too often, a trial and a control are done a very limited number of times—perhaps just once. This is a particular issue when it comes to complex experiments—and what is more complex than a full-scale brew? Say that you want to assess, for instance, the impact of brewing with two different malts (perhaps malts with different levels of lipoxygenase [LOX]) to see how it affects flavor instability. It's a long way from the mill to the beer at the end of forced aging, with innumerable stages in between where batch-to-batch inconsistencies will arise. Too often, I suspect, a single trial and its attendant control are performed, the beers are tasted as described earlier, the data duly come out that the freshness is a little better for the trial, and then whoosh, the paper is published and dogma duly established. If, however, the trial and control brews are

Chapter 4

Evaluating Flavor Change: By Taste and Smell

Chapter 4

Evaluating Flavor Change: By Taste and Smell

done 10 times each and the statistical reporting of tasting work is done properly, then things will not be quite so clear-cut.

There is a further still more fundamental point. Let's look again at the data in Table 4-1 and imagine that we are not talking about freshness but rather haze. Let's say that the scale is 1 "bright," 2 "slightly hazy," 3 "significantly hazy," 4 "very hazy," and 5 "chicken soup." On this basis, we wouldn't think that any of the beers was any darned good.

Herein is the key issue: We are talking about **stability.** In other words, our primary concern is how long our beer can remain on the shelf. The **intensity** of the staleness, while not unimportant, is secondary. Thus, we should be measuring the life of the beer on a scale of time first and intensity of aged character second. That's what happens in studies of haze life. For example, we do forced aging and see how many cycles a beer will tolerate before it becomes unacceptably turbid. (We will look at this more in the next volume on clarity.) (Now, let me "fess up": In many of our studies over the years, we, too, have focused on intensity of staleness rather than how long a product survived before a flavor difference was noted.)

Perhaps an analogy might help. Let's say the thing that keeps you awake at night is not worrying about your beer aging but rather the noise made by a bunch of yowling cats outside your bedroom window. It doesn't matter whether it's one or five or whatever number; you're not resting easy. You want to get those cats, no matter how many, as far away as possible so that you can't hear them. In other words, it's not the amount of noise (cf. the intensity of the staleness) but rather an issue of putting the problem as far away as possible (cf. the time it takes for a stale character to arise). Yes, one cat is better than five, but you still aren't sleeping.

How, then, can we realistically assess flavor life? The simplest way to view the problem is that we want to know how long it takes for a significant difference to appear in the flavor of a beer. On this basis, the approach should be first to decide whether the investigation is going to be done with natural aging or forced aging. This presupposes that there is something that can be fairly described as "natural" aging. If we say that is room temperature, then we have to define that. Perhaps that is an air-conditioned room at, say, 20°C (68°F).

As we saw in Chapter 3, that is a reasonable basis on which to found things. Remember what we said about one beer being labeled with a born-on date and a warning to avoid going beyond 110 days?

So, let's say we base our storage trial on that temperature. Then probably the most reasonable approach is to take samples on a weekly basis of beer stored at that temperature and the same beer stored at 0°C (32°F) before doing a difference test (see volume 2) to ascertain if there is a significant variation between them. In the previously mentioned hypothetical example with the antioxidants (simplifying this to just one antioxidant), then we would have four sets of stored beer: the control beer (no addition) at (a) 20°C and at (b) 0°C and the trial beer (antioxidant added) at (c) 20°C and (d) 0°C. At weekly intervals, we would compare (a) with (b) and (c) and (d) and thereby discover the number of weeks before a significant difference was observed. If the antioxidant had any benefit, that significant difference should occur *later* than for the control beer.

The whole thing could be speeded up by aging at 30°C (86°F), but then we would probably need to do the difference tests at least twice a week.

Naturally, if we are seeking descriptive information on the nature of the flavor changes for a given beer, then we would need to use trained tasters in these trials.

Chapter 4

Evaluating Flavor Change: By Taste and Smell

Analytical Approaches to the Study of Flavor Instability

Chapter 5

A diversity of instrumental methods have been applied to the pursuit of flavor stability in beer. Individually, most of these techniques offer some information, but no single method totally informs the brewer of the full story when it comes to predicting shelf life. Some of the procedures—notably, the measurement of oxygen in packaged beer—certainly have substantial importance. However, most of them tell only part of the story (at best). They are probably best considered as investigative tools: procedures to use when you are troubleshooting or trying to get a handle on where undesirable changes are occurring in the process stream.

The Measurement of Oxygen

I can do no better than refer to the late and greatly missed Chaz Benedict for the plainest description of oxygen measurement, published posthumously (Benedict, 2016).

Above all else, it is essential that measurement is made "in real time." Oxygen will frequently react rapidly with components of wort and beer (or indeed, the likes of yeast), and so the only reliable means of assessing whether oxygen has entered the process is by measuring it as soon as possible.

Chapter 5

Analytical Approaches to the Study of Flavor Instability

A range of oxygen analyzers and sensors are available (Figs. 5-1 through 5-5). The myriad challenges involved in using them reliably are described extensively by Benedict (2016), making his chapter essential reading.

Fig. 5-1. An oxygen analyzer attached in-line in a brewery. (Photo courtesy of Hach)

Fig. 5-2. An in-line oxygen probe. (Photo courtesy of Hach)

Fig. 5-3. An at-line oxygen measurement being made using a portable dissolved oxygen analyzer. (Photo courtesy of Hach)

Chapter 5

Analytical Approaches to the Study of Flavor Instability

Chapter 5

Analytical Approaches to the Study of Flavor Instability

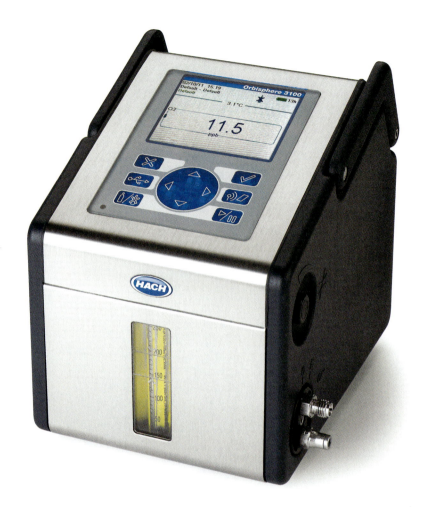

Fig. 5-4. A portable dissolved oxygen analyzer. (Photo courtesy of Hach)

Redox Potential

One way to consider the impact of oxygen (i.e., to assess the extent to which it has encroached without being in a position to measure it directly) is to assess redox potential. Sidebar 3-1 describes the concept of oxidation and reduction. The measurement of the overall balance of oxidation and reduction can be quantified as redox potential, as described by van Strien (1987).

Chapter 5

Analytical Approaches to the Study of Flavor Instability

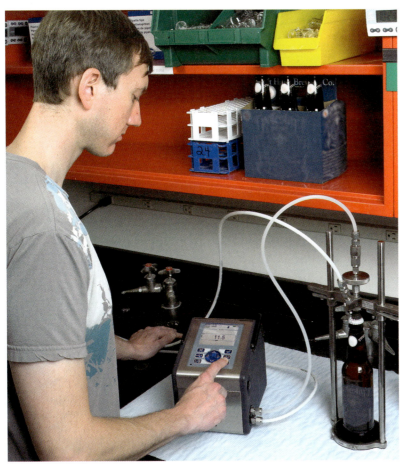

Fig. 5-5. Oxygen measurement for a bottle of beer. (Photo courtesy of Hach)

Redox probes are commercially available (but see my comments in Chapter 6).[1]

If you insist on gaining some idea of how much reducing power has been siphoned away from your process stream, then some of the following simple tests may give clues.

---

[1] I well recall true gentleman Preston Besford, part of the quality team at the Bass Preston Brook Brewery in the late 1980s, asking me whether he could purchase some redox probes. I replied, "But Preston, you have two already. One is here"—and I pointed to one eye—"and there is another one just like it on the other side." My meaning was that simple observation can tell you so much about where oxygen is creeping into a process stream. Is a mash tun being filled by splashing in from the top of the vessel? Oxygen is being picked up, more so than with a gentle bottom fill, and so on.

Chapter 5

Analytical Approaches to the Study of Flavor Instability

The Indicator Time Test

The indicator time test dates back to 1939 and measures the so-called reducing power in wort or beer. The sample is mixed with a blue solution of something called *2,6-dichlorophenolindophenol* (DCPIP). The more reducing power in the sample, the more extensively the blue color is removed.

The TBA Test

In the food industry over the years, there has been much use of thiobarbituric acid (TBA), which can react with carbonyl compounds to generate a pink color. The pinker the color that develops, the more carbonyl substances that are present. And so the test can be used with force-aged samples (perhaps by heating): The more color that develops in the heated sample, the more potential carbonyls that are present in the sample and the less the predicted stability.

This is method Wort-21 of the American Society of Brewing Chemists (ASBC) Methods of Analysis. There have been many criticisms of the method because of the interference of things such as browning reaction products, proteins and sugar degradation products, and amino acids.

Measurement of Thiols

One class of materials that are known to be oxidized relatively easily are the thiols—that is, those substances that contain an –SH grouping. Oxygen removes the hydrogen from two adjacent thiol compounds, causing them to link (see Fig. 5-6). The more oxygen has reacted, the less free –SH can be detected. The regent used to measure the thiols is called *5,5´-dithiobis(2-nitrobenzoic acid)* (DTNB). When an –SH reacts with DTNB, a yellow color develops. The more yellow the color, the more thiol and the less oxidation. (See Muller [1997] for more about this method.)

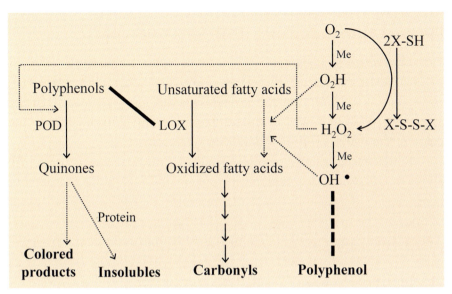

Fig. 5-6. Some of the reactions that may occur in mashing. The abbreviation *POD* stands for *peroxidase.* The bold solid line indicates that polyphenols are said to inhibit lipoxygenase (LOX). The bold dotted line indicates that polyphenol can scavenge reactive oxygen species, such as hydroxyl. (Drawing by Emily Kultgen; Courtesy C. W. Bamforth)

Nonenal Potential

The measurement of nonenal potential involves a forcing test in which wort is adjusted to the typical beer pH (4.0) before heating for a couple of hours at 100°C (212°F) in an atmosphere of argon to exclude oxygen. Then the level of nonenal is measured. As such, the method measures the amount of nonenal that might be lurking in wort—either in the form of precursor that can be converted into nonenal or in the form of nonenal attached to a molecule or molecules that can hold on to it.

Total Polyphenols

By measuring the total polyphenol level, it is possible to get a rough indication of how much has been lost to oxidation. Clearly, this could not be used with beers treated with polyvinyl polypyrrolidone (PVPP). (See ASBC Method Beer-35.)

Chapter 5

Analytical Approaches to the Study of Flavor Instability

Chapter 5
Analytical Approaches to the Study of Flavor Instability

Electron Spin Resonance (ESR) Spectroscopy

Electron spin resonance (ESR) spectroscopy (sometimes referred to as *EPR*) has attracted a lot of attention since the 1990s, and of all the techniques mentioned in this chapter (other than the measurement of oxygen in beer), it is perhaps the most relevant. It, too, warrants an entry in the ASBC Methods (Beer-46).

ESR is basically a way to measure the reactive materials that I talk about in Chapter 3, reactive oxygen species (ROS), or the presence of the materials that lead to the production of ROS. And so a good friend of mine in the industry tells me that ESR is a great way to detect iron. Alternatively, some brewers claim that this method detects the antioxidant potential of a beer.

In the ESR method, a signal is produced for which the intensity is proportional to the amount of these reactive materials (also known as *radicals*). In the procedure, the signal is measured as the beer is force-aged—for example, at 60°C (140°F) (see Chapter 3). This produces the damaging materials (the ROS/radicals). The more antioxidant materials in a beer (materials that grab hold of these radicals and thereby neutralize their damaging impact), the more slowly the signal starts to increase—and the longer the so-called lag time.

For much more detail on the use of ESR in analyzing flavor stability issues, the reader can dip into an online ASBC workshop (see "Further Reading").

The Key Disagreement: How Important Is Upstream Oxidation?

Chapter 6

If you patrol the scientific papers devoted to the topic of upstream oxidation in brewing (referred to by some folks as *hot-side aeration* [HSA], a term that I personally dislike), then you will encounter just as many papers that say it's irrelevant as say that it must be avoided if good flavor stability is to be achieved.

I believe that the answer to the conundrum revolves around the issue that I describe in Chapter 4 regarding the statistical robustness of the sensory approaches that most researchers use. Those folks who have done few replicate brews and who report data in less-than-statistically significant ways may well find that there is a marginally lower staling score when they exclude oxygen in the brewhouse. Others applying the same approaches may conclude the opposite. It's all predicated on a lack of robust experimental technique.

However, let's step aside from repeating these criticisms and discuss the current thinking in various quarters. And let's start in the malt house.

During the germination of barley, there is a clear increase in the level of lipoxygenase (LOX). Indeed, if this enzyme should be the focus of our efforts to greatly enhance flavor stability (see Chapter 3), then there might be a real argument for using unmalted barley, because there is no LOX prior to malting! But let's not go there.

Chapter 6

The Key Disagreement: How Important Is Upstream Oxidation?

It has been shown that alongside the increase in LOX during germination, there are also measureable increases in the levels of oxidized fatty acids, which we have seen are able to break down to give E-2-nonenal (Chapter 3). However, it has also been shown that on kilning, while there is a substantial decrease in the level of LOX, there is a total elimination of oxidized fatty acids. To the best of my understanding, nobody has confirmed exactly what happens to them. Are they converted into entities that are driven off with the vapors on the kiln, in which case they are irrelevant to subsequent brewing? Or are they converted into another form that is lurking in the malt, ready to wreak havoc in the beer in the shape of potential stale character?

Clearly, some brewers believe the latter and are convinced that some malts lead to more stable beers than others. Again, I plead for using a thorough approach that is statistically significant (Chapter 4) before beating up the maltsters for yet another supposed failure.

And so let's move on to sweet wort production. The argument continues with the belief of some that surviving LOX continues its job in the mash, producing oxidized fatty acids that break down to give E-2-nonenal and that this becomes bound up with proteins to form adducts, much as sulfur dioxide binds carbonyl-containing substances (see Chapter 3). The contention continues that these proteins enter into the beer and over time release the nonenal, leading to staling. In other words, the staling potential is established upstream, which is why even beers that are packaged with minute quantities of oxygen go stale.

I have argued that, in fact, unsaturated fatty acids can be oxidized even in the absence of LOX (again, see Chapter 3) and that **if** this is indeed a problem upstream, then minimizing the oxygen ingress in wort production would be the right thing to do. There would be little point in worrying about LOX specifically. However, I have also pointed out that in beer (in which, of course, there is never any LOX), the tiny amounts of unsaturated fatty acid present are still 100,000 times more than are needed to produce stale character, if indeed the oxidation of these materials is the key problem.

Other brewers also argue that oxygen in the brewhouse causes the oxidation of carrier molecules, which are the true oxidizing entities that carry forward to cause oxidation, rather than oxygen itself (see Sidebar 3-1). Possible candidates include so-called thiol substances (molecules containing –SH groups), which cycle between the –SH and the S-S forms in the manner illustrated in Figure 3-6. A further argument is that oxygen in the brewhouse is consumed by various molecules (notably, polyphenols) and that they are then lost to the brew, lowering the antioxidant capacity in the finished product.

The reality is that, indeed, levels of polyphenols and thiols are lowered through the action of oxygen; this is captured in Figure 5-6. The proposal is that oxygen reacts with thiols, which are either in proteins or smaller molecules, with the production of hydrogen peroxide. This is a very active molecule, which of itself is damaging, but it can react with polyphenols either nonenzymically or through the agency of peroxidases to produce oxidized polyphenols. Initially, a reddish-brown color is produced, which is a major concern for those brewers producing light-colored beers, and hence, this is their main reason for wanting to exclude as much oxygen as possible from the brew. Then the polyphenols join together, react with proteins in the mash, and precipitate out. This means that there are significant losses of protein and polyphenol in sweet wort production.

So to recap, the arguments for excluding oxygen from a mash are as follows:

- so that unsaturated fatty acids are not going to be oxidized, either through LOX or nonenzymically
- so that we keep the thiols in the –SH form, meaning that they are not in an oxidizing state
- so that we minimize the loss of polyphenols, which are antioxidants and therefore desirable in beer
- so that we don't develop color

Proponents for avoiding HSA also insist that the precautions should carry forward into the wort boil and hot-wort stand. For my part, I like to remind folks about a long-standing practice from a major brewing company—namely, wort stripping—in which still very, very hot wort is purged using a stream of air to drive off unwanted volatiles (notably, dimethyl sulfide). By the precepts of HSA, this would be a disaster, but the reality is that the famous beer in question is perhaps the cleanest in the marketplace. How can this be?

I think the answer lies in yeast. Yeast loves to reduce carbonyl substances. If you take a beer with pronounced cardboard/wet paper character and treat it with a good virile yeast, the stale notes will be removed. Acetaldehyde is a carbonyl substance, and as we all know, yeast reduces it to ethanol (for which we are very grateful). Diacetyl contains two carbonyl groups, and yeast reduces them both, thereby removing

Chapter 6

The Key Disagreement: How Important Is Upstream Oxidation?

Chapter 6

The Key Disagreement: How Important Is Upstream Oxidation?

the noxious butterscotch/popcorn character (for which most of us are very grateful). Yeast will also reduce E-2-nonenal and other contributors to aged character, and it's for that very reason that I personally question the significance of upstream oxidation. Some argue that the carbonyls are not available to be reduced because they are attached either to proteins (see earlier discussion) or sulfur dioxide. However, that attachment is reversible—and yeast will eventually "do the business" (see Fig. 6-1).

I believe that it's when the yeast has been removed that the liquid stream is at its most vulnerable. And that's why I worry far more about the pickup of oxygen (and metal ions that will "activate" the oxygen, such as iron, copper, and manganese) **after** the yeast has been removed. And it's why I rather like the concept of natural conditioning in the container.

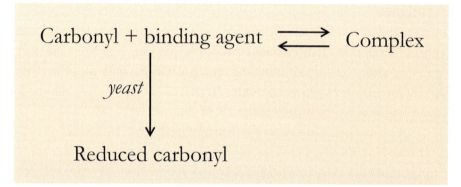

Fig. 6-1. Yeast can reduce carbonyl compounds but only if those carbonyls are not attached to something else (an adduct; see Fig. 3-8). However, the binding of a carbonyl to something such as sulfur dioxide or amino groups in proteins is reversible. There is an equilibrium, and at any one time, some of the carbonyl is in the unattached form. If that free carbonyl is removed by yeast, then more of the carbonyl will be released by the adduct, and that in turn will be removed by the yeast, and so on. Effectively, the yeast is dragging the carbonyl off the adduct. (Drawing by Emily Kultgen; Courtesy C. W. Bamforth)

Strategies for Minimizing Flavor Change

Chapter 7

The way I tell the story is that in 2003, I was asked to give a talk at a national meeting about critical control points for flavor stability and stood up and said, "Keep oxygen out of the package and keep the beer cold. Are there any questions?" There's probably a wee bit of artistic license in this tale, but most assuredly, that was the simple theme of what I had to say.

I do recall some disgruntled faces. One chap stood up and asked, "So what do you say to those people who have invested heavily on brewhouses that minimize oxygen ingress?"

I replied, "Have you also financed refrigerated distribution and warehousing? Have you also armed yourselves with state-of-the-art packaging lines that give filled containers containing the lowest practical oxygen levels? Because if not, you have wasted your money."

There is no getting away from it: Realistic improvements to the flavor life of beer start with the customer. Any brewer seeking to ensure enhanced flavor stability should start there and work back. I sincerely believe that keeping beer fresh is one thing for which the maltster is the very last person to blame.

So, in the rhetoric of this chapter, I am going to start from the end and work back (if not in Table 7-1, which distills some of the relevant actions to minimize oxidative damage, as proposed by various people from time to time—see later in this chapter).

Chapter 7
Strategies for Minimizing Flavor Change

In the table, I point out in bold type those things that I personally feel warrant action, while offering the thought that some of the others **may** have some degree of benefit. Remember, too, that this table does not include other ways in which flavor may change with time—for example, in beers in which the brewer has contrived to leave vicinal diketone precursors in the beer, which break down to release diacetyl and pentanedione over time (see volume 2 in this series). Neither does the table refer to the scalping of hop oils onto the liners of crown corks, thereby leading to a diminution of dry hop character—a problem logically addressed by the evaluation of different packaging materials in pursuit of those that have the least affinity for those aroma substances. I know that there are other possible changes that will not have an a priori solution in this table. It's the way things are: The topic is complex (or do you disagree?). It's why the simple expedient of keeping the beer cold, keeping out oxygen, and drinking it young overwhelms everything else.

So, let's walk backward, as it were, in consideration of flavor instability.

The Customer

Ultimately, substantial responsibility lies with consumers if they are to enjoy a beer with the characteristics that you expect them to appreciate. Consider that most other types of products that enter a home come with some sort of instructions on how to use them and get the most out of them. I see no reason that this should be any different for beer. In short, the drinker needs to be instructed on how best to store a beer for prolonged shelf life (i.e., above all else, cold though not frozen). He or she needs to understand that it does not make sense to purchase beer by the truck load (no matter if there is a certain appeal in that notion for you as the brewer).

Hence, I am a great believer in the concept of a realistic and genuine best-before date (or born-on date, if you want)—one that's established on the basis of flavor acceptability rather than any other criterion (such as appearance), for it's the flavor that will deviate from acceptability fastest of all. So all of this comes down to informative labeling: when to consume by, how to store, and extending, if you like, to best drinking temperature for this style and so on. But with an eye to those imperatives of time and temperature, then perhaps a small table is needed that indicates maximum shelf life if the beer is to be stored at a given temperature (see Table 3-1)—a version that lists, say, refrigerator temperature (4°C [39°F]), classic room temperature (20°C [68°F]), and summer garage temperature (40°C [104°F]). An investment in the label would be a better "spend" than anaerobic processing in the brewhouse.

A word at this point, however, about those beers that actually **benefit** from aging. Included among these are the more alcoholic brews, such as barley wines. One can sample vertically aged beers of this type at some locations. Of course, if we were wine makers, we would be tolerant of aging in any of our products. They wouldn't say "tomcat pee"; rather, they would say "feline." And "wet paper" would be "moist parchment." So you might like to try celebrating flavor instability. It would certainly be an easier option than trying to prevent aging, though I must say it does not appeal to me as a strategy.

The Retailer

I recall being on a flight once and finding myself sitting next to someone from a well-known grocery chain that was notorious for not refrigerating its beer. I registered my dismay at that, which suddenly put an end to the cordial chit-chat.

As at all stages downstream—retail shelf, restaurant, home—there needs to be a simple rule of always selling stock in inverse relation to the age of the beer (Fig. 7-1). I was in a restaurant once and elected to have a beer known for boldly stating its packaging date. "I'd like a young one, please"—a request that clearly perplexed the waiter. Along it came—a beer about 3 months beyond its allotted lifespan. We all know what happened: The beer was emptied from a shelf or refrigerator but not completely, so when the next consignment arrived, it was thoughtlessly used to stock the shelves without any consideration for the older stuff that remained in the back. It really is very simple: stock rotation, whether on the cabinet shelves, in the cellar, wherever.

Warehousing and Distribution

One word: *cold*. It's not that difficult, though it's expensive and it does constitute a hefty slice of the carbon footprint of beer.

Chapter 7

Strategies for Minimizing Flavor Change

Chapter 7

Strategies for Minimizing Flavor Change

Fig. 7-1. Retailers should rotate stock to ensure that beer is sold in inverse relation to its age. (Courtesy Trong Nguyen/Shutterstock.com)

Production

Table 7-1 summarizes my thinking. As noted earlier, I have highlighted in bold type what I think are first-tier considerations. I think these areas are absolutely critical. Italic type indicates the next level of investigation; these items are only to be considered when the bold items have been looked after. The rest: I'm not convinced these are things to think unduly about in the consideration of improving flavor stability.

Table 7-1.

A checklist for improving the flavor stability of beer[a]

Area of Focus	Possibilities
1. Grist selection	1a. **Use malt from lipoxygenase- (LOX-) free barleys.** 1b. Use malts from "traditional" varieties that have been kilned to the highest possible curing temperature consistent with desired color, thereby lessening the level of LOX entering the mash. Maillard-reaction products in such malts may also be antioxidants. 1c. Use adjuncts (e.g., germ-free rice or corn grits; sugars and syrups) that lack unsaturated fatty acids.
2. Sweet wort production	2a. **Less aggressive milling leads to less diminution of embryo tissue and less extensive release of LOX and lipids.** 2b. **Milling under inert gas (nitrogen) lessens air ingress.** 2c. *Purging of air from milled grist with nitrogen is probably more practical than option 2b as a means of ensuring that low oxygen levels enter a mash.* 2d. **De-aerate brewing water (for mashing/sparging), using either an inert gas stream, preboiling, or membrane system designed to remove oxygen.** 2e. *Mixing of milled grist and brewing water using a premasher (cf. Steel's masher) will allow for less air ingress than mixing using a rouser or paddle.* 2f. Avoiding a low temperature stand and mashing straight in at starch conversion temperatures will minimize LOX action. This speaks to the use of homogenously well-modified malt and would also be a reasonable argument for the use of exogenous, heat-stable β-glucanases and xylanases as a solution to removing surviving problematic polysaccharides. 2g. *Mashing at a lower pH (<5.2) will lessen LOX activity.* 2h. **The risk of air ingress increases whenever wort or beer is transferred between vessels. Thus, the fewer the number of transfers and pumping events, the better.**[b] This would argue in favor of avoiding decoction mashing, for example; see also option 2f. Pumps should also be turned off when transfer is complete, and it is imperative that these pumps are properly maintained and do not leak. 2i. *More air is whipped in when a mash is splashed into a vessel from above than when filling is gentle and flows into the base of a vessel. Furthermore, rousers should not be activated until covered.*[b] 2j. *Copper from copper surfaces will dissolve in wort and will induce the production of damaging radicals.*[b] *Copper is pretty, but it only needs to be on the outer surface and not on the inside of the vessel.*

continued

---

[a] Bold = first-tier considerations; italic = second-tier considerations; roman = third-tier considerations.
[b] Also applies at other stages in the process.

Table 7-1. continued

A checklist for improving the flavor stability of beer[a]

Area of Focus	Possibilities
2. Sweet wort production (*continued*)	2k. *For movement of fluid entities (mash, etc.) using a motor gas, the latter should not be air but rather nitrogen.* 2l. *Research has suggested that ascorbic acid added to the mash will scavenge oxygen via an enzyme-catalyzed reaction (ascorbic acid oxidase).*
3. Boiling	3a. *Vigorous boiling will purge off volatile stale substances that may be present as a result of malting or mashing.* 3b. *However, heat induces the production of aging substances such as certain Maillard products (e.g., furfural) and Strecker aldehydes, and there will be a balance between the production and elimination of them. This consideration should focus attention on efficient stripping of volatiles (e.g., as induced by turbulence or, in some more modern systems, a flow of gas) and most assuredly avoidance of a stagnant simmer type of boil.*
4. Hops/Hop products	4a. *Trans isomers of iso-α-acids are more prone to degradation to staling compounds than are cis isomers. The ratio of cis:trans is 2:1 for conventional boiling with hops or pellets but 5:1 for isomerized extracts, so the latter may offer a degree of increased stability. However, there remains a belief that extracts give a lower quality of bitterness in fresh beer.* 4b. *Reduced iso-α-acids that are used for light-resistant beers do not produce unsaturated carbonyl substances, which contribute to staling.*
5. Yeast and fermentation	5a. **The argument has been made that unbound staling substances produced in the brewhouse will be eliminated by the action of yeast (i.e., yeast reduces carbonyl-containing compounds). Good yeast husbandry (e.g., correct pitching rates, healthy yeast) is commensurate with better scavenging of carbonyls.** 5b. *Yeast also produces sulfur dioxide (SO_2), which binds the carbonyl substances that are substantially responsible for aged character in beer. To increase SO_2, increase the sulfate supply to the yeast, increase wort clarity, decrease the oxygenation of wort, reduce the pitching rate, and reduce fermentation temperature.* 5c. *Beer is progressively more susceptible to staling as the pH decreases from 4.5 to 4.0. Therefore, consider moving the pH up in this range (i.e., higher out of fermenter pHs).*

continued

Table 7-1. continued

A checklist for improving the flavor stability of beer[a]

Area of Focus	Possibilities
6. Cold conditioning	6a. **This is a valuable stage for ensuring that the beer has its lowest possible content of oxygen; the use of hydrophobic membrane technology is one possibility.**
7. Dry hopping	7a. *This technique can introduce manganese (also iron and copper) into the beer. Hops and hop products should be screened to select those that release fewer ions.*
8. Filtration and stabilization	8a. *Filter aids may contain iron. Select low-iron options. Also consider using filter-aid-free technologies.* 8b. **Slurry the filter aid (and any other downstream additions) in de-aerated water.** 8c. **Divert the water used to precoat filters to drain; it may contain iron.** 8d. *Control the SO_2 level to the highest level achievable without the risk of exceeding legal imperatives. In the United States, greater than 10mg/L (ppm) must be labeled as "Contains sulfites." A reasonable "safe" target is 7 ppm.*
9. Packaging	9a. **Use double evacuation, inert gases, tappers and jetters, undercover gassing, and other low-air filling protocols; in summary, install state-of-the-art low-air-packaging equipment.** 9b. **Use pry-off rather than twist-off crown corks. Pay attention to seals.** 9c. *Oxygen-scavenger crown corks are available.* 9d. **The oxygen levels achievable in packaging cans are a little higher than can be achieved for bottles; however, there is no air ingress into a can with time.** 9e. *Yeast in bottle-conditioned beer affords some protection by scavenging carbonyl substances.*
10. Final product	10a. **Store and transport beer as cold as possible (short of freezing) and with the least possible agitation.** 10b. **Practice proper stock rotation such that beer is moved for consumption in age sequence: Drink the oldest first.**

Light Instability: Skunking

Chapter **8**

Born and raised in England, I had never smelled a skunk before I came to live in California in 1999. (There are no skunks in England.) So, in the land of my fathers and mothers, the word *skunky* means nothing. But we sure know something is happening to our beer when it sees light. We describe it using words such as *sun-struck* and *light-struck,* but *skunky* is so much more evocative, don't you think?

Before we get too deep into lamentations surrounding this particular issue, we must not lose sight of the fact that some folks like this smell. I have a South African friend who grew up adoring the skunk-like smell of a certain plant, to the extent that she will drive out to the site of a skunk's demise just to inhale. I might also simply draw attention to the whiff of hybrids of *Cannabis sativa* and *C. indica*. Get the drift?

Maybe most folks don't even notice the scent as they relax in the beer garden on a pleasing afternoon, slowly sipping on a glass of beer. By the time they are midglass, that beer smells like the backside of the black-and-white critter. There's nothing to be done about this (short of the modified hop route, which I'll return to momentarily). You could always drink in the dark!

The problem is caused by light of wavelengths in the lower visible end of the spectrum (the blue end) and higher wavelengths in the ultraviolet (UV) region. The light is captured by one of the B vitamins,

Chapter 8

Light Instability: Skunking

riboflavin, and the energy is duly transferred to the bitter acids (the iso-α-acids). A bit of the molecule snaps off and reacts with traces of sulfur (the source of which is uncertain), and the product is 3-methyl-2-butene-1-thiol, which you will be glad to hear I am going to henceforth call *MBT*. This is the source of the skunk smell.

And MBT sure is potent. Some people can detect it at a level of 4 parts per trillion. Think about it: If we were talking about the distance to Mars (on average, 140 million miles [225 million km]), 4 parts in 1 trillion would represent a distance of ½ mile (0.8 km) on that journey.

What this means is that you really don't need very much of a breakdown of bitter acids to get the problem. Even beers with only a soupçon of bitterness have vastly more MBT potential than one might wish for.

Assuming that we want to avoid this character, the simplest expedient is to keep beer out of the light—and I mean any white light. Even beer displayed in illuminated cabinets will go skunky, depending on the nature of the package.

Cans? No problem: Light is not going to get in. Brown glass? The best, as sustained exposure to light is required for beer in these bottles to deteriorate, though deteriorate it will (Fig. 8-1). But that won't happen anywhere nearly as quickly as if the beer is in green or flint (clear) glass bottles. The marketing folks think these bottles are sexier than brown glass receptacles, but the technical folks (as usual) know best.

Say, though, that the marketers hold sway. How, then, to prevent the catastrophe? (This presupposes that this is your intent—to prevent the skunking of beer.) You could always accept skunking and simply encourage people to consume your brand by convincing them that they will look beautiful on the beach, provided they shove a wedge of lime in the neck of the bottle.

Some folks have suggested using proteins that specifically grab hold of riboflavin to prevent it from snatching the light. However, the only commercial reality is the use of so-called reduced side-chain iso-α-acids: bitter substances to which hydrogen has been added. These substances no longer produce MBT. They were pioneered by a major U.S. company celebrated for its clear glass bottles. The process involves extracting the α-acids from hop powder using very cold carbon dioxide, isomerizing the molecules using a salt, and then adding hydrogen over a palladium catalyst.

This process works for the most part, although scientists from this company have shown that such beers still deteriorate in the light

Chapter 8

Light Instability: Skunking

Fig. 8-1. Brown glass is superior to both green glass and clear glass in blocking exposure to light. (Courtesy William Allum/Shutterstock.com)

through other mechanisms. Another downside is that the foams of the beers bittered using these materials can be less appealing than those of the beers bittered in more traditional ways (see *Foam,* volume 1 in this series).

It is also important to realize that there must be absolutely no unreduced iso-α-acid in these beers. The tiniest quantity will produce skunking; see what I said earlier. Bitter molecules will cling onto surfaces, and while clean-in-place (CIP) systems should remove most of them, there is always the risk that enough will survive. And absolutely any yeast that has seen a regular iso-α-acid must never be used to ferment a beer that is going to be bittered using the reduced substances downstream.

Further Reading

Chapter 1

Guinard, J.-X., Uotani, B., and Schlich, P. (2001) Internal and external mapping of preferences for commercial lager beers: Comparison of hedonic ratings by consumers blind versus with knowledge of brand and price. Food Qual. Pref. 12:243–255.

Stephenson, W. H., and Bamforth, C. W. (2002) The impact of light-struck and stale character in beers on their perceived quality: A consumer study. J. Inst. Brew. 108:406–409.

Chapter 2

Bamforth, C. W. (2000) Making sense of flavor change in beer. MBAA Tech. Q. 37:165–171.

Bushnell, S. E., Guinard, J.-X., and Bamforth, C. W. (2003) Effects of sulfur dioxide and polyvinylpolypyrrolidone (PVPP) on the flavor stability of beer as measured by sensory and chemical analysis. J. Am. Soc. Brew. Chem. 61:133–141.

Further Reading

Chapter 3

Bamforth, C. W. (1999) The science and understanding of the flavour stability of beer: A critical assessment. Brauwelt Int. 17:98–110.

Bamforth, C. W. (2006) Scientific Principles of Malting and Brewing. American Society of Brewing Chemists, St. Paul, MN.

Bamforth, C. W. (2010) Flavour changes in beer: Oxidation and other pathways. In: Oxidation in Foods and Beverages and Antioxidant Applications. Vol 2, Management in Different Industry Sectors. E. Decker, R. Elias, and D. J. McClements, eds. Woodhead, Cambridge, U.K. pp. 424–444.

Ilett, D. R., and Simpson, W. J. (1995) Loss of sulfur dioxide during storage of bottled and canned beers. Food Res. Int. 28:393–396.

Vanderhaegen, B., Neven, H., Verachtert, H., and Derdelinckx, G. (2006) The chemistry of beer aging—A critical review. Food Chem. 95:357–381.

Chapter 4

Bamforth, C. W., and Lentini, A. (2009) The flavour instability of beer. In: Beer: A Quality Perspective. C. W. Bamforth, ed. Academic Press, Boston. pp. 85–109.

Meilgaard, M. (2001) Effects on flavour of innovations in brewery equipment and processing: A review. J. Inst. Brew. 107:271–286.

Chapter 5

American Society of Brewing Chemists (ASBC). (n.d.) Free Radicals, Antioxidants, and EPR Metrics. B. Foster, presenter. Available online: http://methods.asbcnet.org/training.aspx

Benedict, C. S. (2016) Dissolved gases. In: Brewing Materials and Processes: A Practical Approach to Beer Excellence. C. W. Bamforth, ed. Academic Press, Boston. pp. 157–174.

Muller, R. (1997) The formation of hydrogen peroxide during oxidation of thiol-containing proteins. J. Inst. Brew. 103:307–310.

van Strien, J. (1987) Direct measurement of the oxidation-reduction condition of wort and beer. J. Am. Soc. Brew. Chem. 45:77–79.

Chapter 6

Bamforth, C. W. (2002) Great brewing debates: Part 5. Beer freshness: Is the maltster to blame? Brew. Guard. 131(11):22–24.

Bamforth, C. W. (2004) A critical control point analysis for flavor stability of beer. MBAA Tech. Q. 41:97–103.

Bamforth, C. W. (2004) Fresh controversy: Conflicting opinions on beer staling. Proc. Conv. IGB Asia-Pacific. pp. 63–73.

Chapter 7

Bamforth, C. W. (2011) 125th anniversary review: The non-biological instability of beer. J. Inst. Brew. 117:488–497.

Chapter 8

Templar, J., Arrigan, K., and Simpson, W. J. (1995) Formation, measurement and significance of lightstruck flavour in beer: A review. Brew. Dig. 70(5):18–25.

Index

acetaldehyde
    as carbonyl, 14, 18, 41
    E-2-nonenal production by, 18
acetolactate, 8
adducts, formation of, 23, 40, 42
aged character
    intensity of, 26, 28
    qualities of, 8, 11, 17, 23, 42
    yeast and, 42, 48
aging
    beneficial effects of, 5, 45
    regimens, 10–11
alcohol content
    aging and, 5, 45
    influence on flavor, 19
alcohols, oxidation of, 17, 18, 19
aldehydes, 17, 48. *See also* carbonyls, compounds containing
American Society of Brewing Chemists (ASBC) Methods of Analysis
    Beer-35, 37
    Beer-46, 38
    Wort-21, 36
amino acids, and carbonyl production, 18
antioxidants
    measurement of, 38, 41
    sample trial involving, 26–28, 29
aroma attributes. *See also* notes
    cardboard character, 5, 8, 12
    descriptive terms for, 8, 9, 10, 11

Arrhenius, Svante August, 21–22
ASBC Methods of Analysis. *See* American Society of Brewing Chemists (ASBC) Methods of Analysis

barley
    germination of, 14, 39, 40
    unsaturated fatty acids in, 14
barley wines, 5, 45
Beer-35 (ASBC Method), 37
Beer-46 (ASBC Method), 38
Benedict, Chaz, 31, 32
Besford, Preston, 35
best-before date, determination of, 1–2, 44. *See also* born-on date
Biosystemes, 10
bitter acids
    decrease during storage, 8
    formation of carbonyls, 17
    forms of, 17
    oxidation of, 17
    skunky flavor and, 51–52
bitterness
    decrease over time, 17, 19
    MBT potential of, 52
    perception of, 7–8
    sweetness and, 7–8
boiling, and improving flavor stability, 48
born-on date, 22, 28, 44. *See also* best-before date

brands/branding
    consistency in flavor, 2
    influence on customers, 2–3
Brewing Research Foundation, 7
Burton (-on-Trent, England), 4
Bushnell, Sarah, 8, 9

carbonyls
    carbonyl groups, 13–14, 41
    compounds containing, 17, 18, 23, 36, 40, 48
    flavor and, 14, 18, 48
    production of, 14, 17, 18
    reduction by yeast, 41–42, 48, 49
    staling effect of, 16, 17
cardboard character
    aging and, 7, 8
    aroma and, 8, 10, 11
    customer preference for, 5
    descriptors of, 10
    development of, 7, 8, 12, 14, 22
    reference standard for, 11
    removal with yeast, 41–42
    temperature and, 12, 22
Carling Black Label, 4
chemical reactions, and temperature, 21–22
CIP systems. *See* clean-in-place (CIP) systems
cis isomers, 17, 48
clean-in-place (CIP) systems, 53
cold conditioning, and improving flavor stability, 49
color (of beer)
    customer preference for, 5
    formation of, 15, 17, 36, 41
consistency, as goal, 6
customers
    color preferences of, 5
    flavor perceptions of, 4–5, 7–8
    influence of branding on, 2–3
    influence of foam on, 3
    storage of beer by, 43, 44–45
    taste expectations of, 2–3, 5–6

Dalgliesh, Charles, 7, 8
DCPIP. *See* 2,6-dichlorophenolindophenol
decoction mashing, 15, 47

diacetyl
    carbonyl groups in, 41–42
    flavor and, 8, 14
    production of, 44
distribution, and temperature, 43, 45, 49
dry hop character, 44
dry hopping, and improving flavor stability, 49
DTNB. *See* 5,5'dithiobis(2-nitrobenzoic acid)

E-2-nonenal
    flavor and, 14
    production of, 7, 12, 14, 18, 40
    reduction by yeast, 42
electron spin resonance (ESR) spectroscopy, 38
EPR. *See* electron spin resonance (ESR) spectroscopy
ESR. *See* electron spin resonance (ESR) spectroscopy
esters
    flavor and, 8, 10, 13
    production of, 18, 19
ethanol, production of, 1
experimental design
    for panel assessment, 10
    robustness of, 25, 28, 39
    for trial evaluations, 25, 27–28, 39

fermentation, and improving flavor stability, 48
filtration, and improving flavor stability, 49
5,5'dithiobis(2-nitrobenzoic acid) (DTNB), 36
5-hydroxymethylfurfural, 17
FIZZ Network Acquisition software, 10
flavor attributes, description of, 9, 10, 11
flavor change(s)
    beer intensity and, 5, 8, 26
    as instability, 8. *See also* flavor instability
    light and. *See* light
    minimization of, 13, 43–49
    oxidation and. *See* oxidation
    pace of, 5, 28
    temperature and. *See* temperature
flavor instability
    carbonyl-containing substances, 18. *See also* carbonyls, compounds containing
    light and, 51–52. *See also* light

    minimization of, 13, 18–19, 43–49
    nature of, 8, 13
    oxidation and, 19. *See also* oxidation
    storage and distribution, 44–45
    study of, 25, 26–29, 31–38
    temperature and. *See* temperature
flavor thresholds, 13
foam
    bitter acids and, 53
    fatty acids and, 14
    influence on customers, 3
forced aging
    in measuring oxygen, 36, 38
    in research studies, 12, 22, 27, 28
freshness
    characters of, 8
    customer expectations and, 5–6
    oxidation and, 14, 19, 25. *See also* oxidation
    refrigeration and, 22. *See also* temperature
    taste trials to evaluate, 2–3
furfural, 17, 48

glass color, and light exposure, 52
grist selection, and improving flavor stability, 47
Guinard, Jean-Xavier, 3, 8, 9

haze
    production of, 19
    ratings of, 28
heptanal, 18
higher alcohols, oxidation of, 17, 18, 19
hops
    aroma attribute, 5, 10, 11
    flavor attribute, 13, 17, 44
    improving flavor stability, 48, 49
    scalping of oils, 8, 44
hot-side aeration (HSA), 39, 41. *See also* upstream oxidation
HSA. *See* hot-side aeration
hydrogen
    oxidation and, 16, 20, 36
    reduction and, 20, 52
hydrogen peroxide, production of, 41

Ilett, David, 23
imino acid, 18
imported beer, customer preferences for, 3
indicator time test, 36

infusion mashing, 14, 15
instrumental methods, 31–38
    electron spin resonance (ESR) spectroscopy, 38
    indicator time test, 36
    nonenal potential measurement, 37
    oxygen measurement, 31–34
    redox potential measurement, 34–35
    TBA test, 36
    thiol measurement, 36
    total polyphenol measurement, 37
intensity
    aged character and, 8, 28
    staleness and, 28
iso-α-acids, 17, 48, 52–53

kilning
    degradation of lipoxygenase, 14, 15, 40
    elimination of oxidized fatty acids, 40
    production of Maillard reaction products, 15
    production of melanoidins, 17
    temperature of, 15, 47

labeling, and recommended storage temperatures, 44–45
light
    flavor change and, 3, 15, 51–53
    glass color and, 52
    production of reactive oxygen species, 15
    wavelengths of, 51–52
linoleic acid, 14, 16
lipid, oxidation of, 14, 16, 21
lipoxygenase (LOX)
    cardboard character and, 7
    degradation/elimination of, 8, 14, 15, 37, 40
    germination of barley and, 39, 40
    heat susceptibility of, 14, 15, 47
    levels in malts, 27, 47
    oxidation of unsaturated fatty acids, 7, 14–15, 40, 41
LOX. *See* lipoxygenase

Maillard reaction products
    definition, 15
    inhibition of lipoxygenase, 15
    staling and, 17–18
    substances produced, 17
MBT. *See* 3-methyl-2-butene-1-thiol
Meilgaard, Morten, 8, 25, 26

melanoidins, 17–18, 19
metal ions, 15, 21, 42

natural aging, 28
nonenal potential, measurement of, 37
notes
    aging conditions and, 12
    aroma, 5, 12
    customer expectations and, 5, 6
    flavor, 7–8, 9, 41. *See also specific flavors/notes*
    flavor change and, 13

Owades, Joe, 18
oxidation
    of alcohols, 17, 18, 19
    of bitter acids, 17
    cardboard character and, 7
    of carrier molecules, 40
    chemistry of, 20
    flavor change and, 3, 7, 19, 20
    of lipids, 21
    of lipoxygenase, 7
    polyphenol measurement and, 37
    redox potential and, 34
    reduction vs., 20, 34
    thiol measurement and, 36
    of unsaturated fatty acids, 7, 14–16, 19, 40, 41
    upstream, 39–42
oxidative damage, minimization of, 43–44, 46, 47–49
oxidized fatty acids. *See* unsaturated fatty acids, oxidation of
oxygen
    active forms of, 15. *See also* reactive oxygen species
    color development and, 41
    exclusion of, 41
    flavor stability and, 12, 19, 21. *See also* oxidation
    measurement of, 31–34
oxygen analyzers/sensors, 32, 33–34

packaging, and improving flavor stability, 49
panel, training of, 9–11
peroxidase (POD), 37, 41
POD. *See* peroxidase
polyphenols
    carbonyl production and, 18
    flavor change and, 9, 18, 41

inhibition of higher alcohols, 17, 18
inhibition of lipoxygenase, 15, 37
    loss of, 41
    measurement of, 37
    oxidation and, 5, 17, 18, 37, 40, 41
    staling and, 9, 41
polyvinyl polypyrrolidone (PVPP), 9, 10, 11, 37
preliminary tasting, 9
Preston Brook Brewery (Bass, England), 4, 35
proline, 18
PVPP. *See* polyvinyl polypyrrolidone

radicals, 38. *See also* reactive oxygen species
reactive oxygen species (ROS)
    measurement of, 38
    melanoidins and, 17–18
    oxidation and, 16, 21
    production of, 15–16
redox chains, 20
redox potential, measurement of, 34–35
redox state, 20
reducing power, 35–36
reduction, 20, 34
refrigeration, and freshness, 22, 45. *See also* temperature
retailers, stock rotation by, 45, 49
ribes character
    development/subsiding of, 8
    oxygen and, 12
riboflavin, and skunky flavor, 52
ROS. *See* reactive oxygen species

SAS Institute, 11
scorecard, for panel assessment, 9, 10
sensory attributes, 9, 10, 11
sensory techniques, 25, 39
side-chain iso-α-acids, 52
Simpson, Bill, 23
skunky flavor, 51–53
sodium metabisulfite, 23
staling/staleness
    assessment of, 2–3, 9–11, 26, 27
    boiling and, 48
    carbonyls and, 16, 17, 48
    customer expectations and, 5–6
    detection of, 19

staling/staleness (cont'd.)
    intensity of, 28
    melanoidins and, 17–18
    nonenal and, 49
    pH and, 15, 48
    sulfites/sulfur dioxide and, 9, 23, 40
    temperature and, 22
    upstream oxidation and, 39–42
    yeast treatment and, 41, 48
Statistical Analysis System (SAS) software, 11
Stephenson, Bill, 2–3
storage
    bitter acid decrease during, 8
    light levels in, 52
    temperature levels in, 12, 44–45, 49
storage trial, 28–29
sulfites, 23, 49
sulfur dioxide, 9, 23, 40, 42, 48
sweet wort production, 40, 41, 47–48
sweetness, and perceived bitterness, 7–8

Talbot, Neil, 4
tannin content, 5
tasters, training of, 9–11, 29
TBA test, 36
temperature
    chemical reactions and, 21–22
    distribution/transport and, 45, 49
    flavor change and, 12, 21–22, 28
    recommendations for customers, 44–45
    staling and, 22
    storage/warehousing and, 17, 29, 44–45, 49
    storage trial and, 29
term-generation sessions, 9
thiobarbituric acid (TBA), 36
thiols
    measurement of, 36
    oxidation of, 36, 41
    substances containing, 20
3-methyl-2-butene-1-thiol (MBT), 52
trans isomers, 17, 48
trans-2-nonenal, 7. *See also* E-2-nonenal
transport, and temperature, 49
trials
    for flavor instability, 26–29
    flawed methods in, 25, 27–29, 39
    for storage, 28–29
    for taste, 2–3
    training panels for, 9–11
2,6-dichlorophenolindophenol (DCPIP), 36

unsaturated fatty acids, 14–17
    oxidation of, 7, 14–16, 19, 40, 41
    types of, 14
upstream oxidation, 39–42

warehousing, and temperature, 45. *See also* storage
West Coast IPAs, 5
wet paper character, 7, 8, 41, 45. *See also* cardboard character
Whitbread (Beer Company), 2
Whitear, Tony, 2
wort
    bitterness and, 19
    carbonyl production and, 14
    degradation of, 14
    nonenal potential measurement and, 37
    oxidation and, 20, 31
    reducing power in, 36
wort boiling, 17, 41
wort stripping, 41
Wort-21 (ASBC Method), 36

yeast
    fermentation and, 18, 48
    improving flavor stability and, 48
    reaction with oxygen, 31
    reduction of carbonyl-containing compounds by, 41–42, 48, 49